PRAYER & STUDY GUIDE

STORMIE OMARTIAN

PRAYER WARRIOR

HARVEST HOUSE PUBLISHERS
EUGENE, OREGON

PRAYER WARRIOR PRAYER AND STUDY GUIDE
Copyright © 2013 by Stormie Omartian
Published by Harvest House Publishers
Eugene, Oregon 97402
www.harvesthousepublishers.com

ISBN 978-0-7369-5369-6 (pbk.)
ISBN 978-0-7369-5370-2 (eBook)

Printed in the United States of America

13 14 15 16 17 18 19 20 21 / BP-CD / 10 9 8 7 6 5 4 3 2

This book belongs to

_____

Please do not read beyond this page
without permission of the person named above.

A supplemental workbook to
Prayer Warrior
by Stormie Omartian

CONTENTS

What You Need to Know
Before You Begin

———◆———

My goal in this *Prayer and Study Guide* is not only to convince you that God has called you to be His prayer warrior, but also to show you how to become the best prayer warrior possible. I want you to take a stand for God's side in the battle between good and evil that is going on around you at all times. I want to help you know your Leader, identify your true enemy, and be convinced of your authority in prayer. You must also know how to condition yourself to be the strongest and best prayer warrior you can be so that you can fight the good fight in prayer. I want you to be certain about how to put on your spiritual armor every day so you are protected and prepared to become skilled with your spiritual weapons. It's important that you are engaged in the war and able to identify the immediate battlefield whenever the enemy attacks. I want you to know how to resist the enemy so that he flees from you and you don't get thrown by his evil tactics.

Finally, I want to help you see things from God's perspective so that you understand what is going on *in* you, *around* you, and *to* you. I not only want to equip you with certain prayers you can pray the moment you need them, but also to help you formulate your own prayers so that they will be a starting point from which you can pray more specifically about the things personally concerning you. These prayers will be there as reminders whenever you need them. The prayers that you write in this book will be put together from Scripture and from your own experience and observations. They will help you to push back the encroachment of the enemy into your life and the lives of others.

Remember that the battle is fought in prayer. You won't get wounded there. Instead, you will be protected. The armor and the weapons of warfare will not only protect you, they will give you great victory over any plans the enemy may have for your life. You're in the war zone anyway, so you might as well be able to not only defend yourself but also push the enemy back from you and your family and the people and situations God is putting on your heart. In doing so, you will be able to advance God's kingdom on earth. When you finish this *Prayer and Study Guide*, you will know with certainty what you are called to do in prayer and how to find the joy of fulfilling that calling for the Lord you love and serve.

You will need the book *Prayer Warrior*, and it will be referred to as "the book" within each week's questions and directions. You will also need your Bible, a notepad, or even better yet a journal or notebook you will want to keep as you write out more and more prayers. I am hoping you will run out of room writing out your prayers in this book because you will be thinking of so many things to pray about.

Don't for a moment let this become overwhelming. You do not have to pray every prayer every day. Not even close to that. Simply follow the leading of the Holy Spirit in you. You might pray just one of the prayers in a day. Or God may put two areas of prayer focus on your heart for days. God knows what He wants you to pray about, and He will show you if you ask Him. Stay close to Him in prayer and be sensitive to His Spirit guiding you. Your relationship with the Lord is about to get closer than ever, and you are going to love sensing His presence in you more and more.

Although this *Prayer and Study Guide* is divided into 12 weeks for group study—which helps people stay on the same page and move together within a specific time frame for completion—if you are doing it alone or with another person, you can move at your own pace in whatever time frame works best for you. Just go with the flow…of the Spirit, that is.

Week One

Read Chapter 1:
"Understand There Is a War and You Are in It"
in *Prayer Warrior*

1. How to Build a Solid Foundation

Read 1 Corinthians 3:11-15. What is the foundation on which we are to build our lives? (verse 11)

_____

_____

Verse 12 says we can build with something that does not perish—such as gold, silver, and precious stones. Or we can build with something that *does* perish—such as wood, hay, and straw. How will it be revealed whether we have built with something that perishes or something that does not perish? (verse 13)

_____

_____

_____

What happens when you build with something that lasts? (verse 14)

_____

_____

What happens if you build with something that does not last? (verse 15)

_____

_____

Read Luke 6:47-49. Where does the person who obeys God build? What happens because he builds there? (verses 47-48)

_____

_____

_____

What happens to the person who does not obey the Lord? (verse 49)

_____

_____

_____

Read Proverbs 10:25. What happens to the wicked and the righteous after the storms of life pass by?

_____

_____

_____

Read 1 Corinthians 10:4. Who is the spiritual Rock?

_____

_____

Read 2 Samuel 22:32. Who is the rock?

_____

_____

Write out a prayer asking God to help you build your life on the solid foundation of Jesus. Tell Him you want to be someone who obeys Him and why.

_____

_____

_____

_____

_____

2. There Is a War Going On

Read James 4:1-3. Where do wars and fighting come from? (verse 1)

_____

_____

_____

What are the two reasons we do not have what we want? (verses 2-3)

_____

_____

_____

3. God's Enemy Is Your Enemy

Read James 4:4. How can you become God's enemy?

_____

_____

Having "friendship with the world" is not talking about the beautiful world God made or the good people He created. It is talking about a world system that is godless and anti-Christ. It is fueled by lust and pride. Have you recognized in your own observations that there are people, businesses, or groups of people who do not welcome the name of Jesus or even forbid it? Explain what you have recognized by writing it out as a prayer concerning those who oppose Him.

_____

_____

_____

_____

Once you understand that a war is going on and you are in it, you must make a decision as to *whose side you are on*. Are you on God's side or the enemy's side? The enemy prowls the world. God is in the heavenly place. Trying to befriend the world's system and values makes you God's enemy. Write out a prayer asking God to help you draw closer to Him and away from the world system that rejects Him. Ask Him to help you be clearly aware of the anti-Christ spirit that is in the world today so that you do not support it in any way.

_____

_____

_____

_____

_____

4. The Heart of a Prayer Warrior

Read from the middle of page 15 to the middle of page 16 in the book, under the same subtitle as above. If you were to answer all the questions posed in that section, in what ways would you have the heart of a prayer warrior?

_____

_____

_____

_____

What does a prayer warrior have? (See page 16 in the book, the fourth paragraph down.)

_____

_____

_____

_____

What is the biggest issue on your heart right now?

_____

_____

_____

_____

What is the biggest issue on your heart concerning the way God is being pushed out of society? Where have you seen the anti-Christ spirit and anti-Christian bias spewed forth? Write out your answer as a prayer to God. (For example, "Lord, I am concerned that children are not allowed to pray in school…")

_____

_____

_____

_____

_____

5. You May Pray Alone but You Don't Fight Alone

Read Romans 8:26. Who helps us to pray and why?

_____

_____

When we pray as prayer warriors, we are not alone because God has called people all over the world to pray as well. Write out a prayer asking God to raise up more and more prayer warriors who will hear His call to pray.

_____

_____

_____

_____

_____

6. The Time Is Later Than We Think

Read Ecclesiastes 9:12, Amos 5:13, and Micah 2:3. What is the common thread in these Scriptures concerning the times?

_____

_____

_____

Read Ephesians 5:15-16. Redeeming the time means to take advantage of the time we have to pray. A time will come when we wish we had prayed about something but we have not. Has there ever been a time you can remember when you wished you had prayed about something but you didn't and then it was too late? Explain. Write out a prayer asking God to prompt you when something is important you should be praying about. Ask Him to give you ears to hear His call.

_____

_____

_____

_____

7. I Don't Want to Be in a War—I Hate Violence

Read 1 Peter 1:6-7. We all have trials in this life. What is a good thing that can come out of our trials?

_____

_____

_____

Write out a prayer asking God to help you pray as a powerful prayer warrior in the midst of difficulties instead of becoming discouraged.

_____

_____

_____

_____

_____

Read 1 Peter 4:12-13. Is it unusual to go through trials? What should we do in the midst of them?

_____

_____

_____

_____

Read James 1:2-4. What should be our reaction to trials, difficult times, or enemy attacks? Why? (verses 2-3)

_____

_____

_____

_____

What can happen when we experience various trials? (verse 4)

_____

_____

_____

_____

8. This Sounds like Too Much Work

Read John 17:4. What does Jesus say about the work God had given Him to do?

_____

_____

_____

Write out a prayer asking God to help you be a great prayer warrior for Him so you can say those same words to the Lord at the end of your life.

_____

_____

_____

_____

_____

Read Galatians 6:2. How does this verse sum up what it means to be a prayer warrior? See also page 23 in the book, the bottom half of the page.

_____

_____

_____

Read Matthew 5:16. Why is it important to let certain people know you are a prayer warrior and you will pray for them?

_____

_____

_____

_____

Week Two

"Know Your Commander and Stand on His Side"
in *Prayer Warrior*

1. Your Commander Chose You

Read Ephesians 1:3-5. When did God choose us and why?

_____

_____

_____

_____

Read 1 Peter 2:9. If you are a believer in Jesus, what does this Scripture say about you?

_____

_____

_____

_____

Do you feel chosen and special? If so, write out a prayer of thanks to God for seeing you that way. If you do not feel chosen by God or special, write out a prayer asking God to help you believe all of the good things He says about you.

_____

_____

_____

_____

_____

2. Your Commander Saves You

Read Romans 10:13. How can you be saved?

_____

_____

Read Romans 10:9. How can you be saved?

_____

_____

Read the following Scriptures and write what they say about being saved.

John 12:47 _____

_____

Acts 4:12 _____

_____

Acts 16:31 _____

_____

1 Timothy 2:3-4 _____

_____

2 Timothy 1:8-9_____

_____

Have you been saved? If so, what was it that drew you to the Lord? What was your experience, and how did that decision change your life?

_____

_____

_____

_____

(If you have never received Jesus, I pray the rest of this text in question 2 will touch your heart. Even if you have received Jesus, read it to know more about how you might lead someone to the Lord.)

The greatest gift God has given us is His Son. He is the ultimate example of the unconditional love of God. Jesus came to earth to lead us to the truth and redeem us from the consequences of our own sins. Because the consequence for sin is death, there must be a death in order to pay for the sin. Jesus gave His life to pay that debt for us, which enables us who receive Him to have a close relationship with God. We were once alienated from God because of sin, but now, because of receiving Jesus, we have been restored into close relationship with God and He sees the righteousness of Jesus in us. We are now holy in His sight. "You, who once were alienated and enemies in your mind by wicked works, yet now He has reconciled in the body of His flesh through death, to present you holy, and blameless, and above reproach in His sight" (Colossians 1:21-22).

When Jesus was resurrected from the dead, He broke the power of death and hell in our lives. The enemy no longer has power over those who have received Jesus. Jesus sent the Holy Spirit—who is also the Spirit of Christ because Jesus and the Father are one God— to live in us and to lead and guide us and change us from the inside out. We are not saved because of how good we are. The Bible says, "By grace you have been saved through faith, and that not of yourselves; it is the gift of God, not of works, lest anyone should boast" (Ephesians 2:8-9). *When we receive Jesus*, the same power that resurrected Him will resurrect us when we die. Jesus said, "I am the resurrection and the life. He who believes in Me, though he may die, he shall live" (John 11:25).

We all need a second chance—a new beginning. The Bible says, "If anyone is in Christ, he is a new creation; old things have passed away; behold, all things have become new" (2 Corinthians 5:17). If you want a chance to begin again and enter into all God has for you, both now and also in eternity, say the following prayer:

> *Lord Jesus, I believe You are the Son of God as You say You are. I believe You laid down Your life on the cross and were resurrected from the dead so that I can have eternal life with You. I confess all my sins and failings, and I repent of any time I have not lived Your way. Thank You for forgiving me. Come into my heart and fill me with Your Spirit so that I can become all You created me to be and spend eternity with You. Help me to live Your way now.*

If you said this prayer, write in the date below so you will always remember this day as the beginning of your walk with the Lord. If you have already received Jesus, write in the date you received Him.

The day I received Jesus is

_____

Whether you just received the Lord or it happened in the past, write out a prayer thanking Him for loving you enough to die for you so that you can dwell in His kingdom both now and forever.

_____

_____

_____

_____

3. Your Commander Makes You a Joint Heir with Him

Read Romans 8:16-17 and Galatians 4:7. If you are a son or daughter of God, then what else are you?

_____

_____

_____

Read Ephesians 1:13-14. What is the guarantee of our inheritance?

_____

_____

Read Colossians 3:24. Why will you receive an inheritance from God?

_____

_____

_____

Read Hebrews 1:13-14. To whom do the angels minister?

_____

_____

Read 1 Peter 1:3-4. How secure is your inheritance in the Lord?

_____

_____

4. Your Commander Gives You His Spirit to Live in You

Read Luke 11:11-13. What does God give us as a gift? Why does He do that?

_____

_____

Read Titus 3:4-5. What does the Holy Spirit do in us?

_____

_____

_____

_____

Read Romans 8:8-9. What is the proof you are the Lord's?

_____

_____

Read Romans 8:11. If the same Spirit who raised Jesus dwells in you, what does that mean for you?

_____

_____

Read Romans 8:16. What does the Holy Spirit do for us?

_____

_____

Read John 14:26. What is another name for the Holy Spirit, and what will He do?

_____

_____

Read John 16:7. Why did Jesus need to go away to His Father God?

_____

_____

5. Your Commander Wants You to Choose His Side

Read Hebrews 12:28-29. Why should we serve God by standing on His side in prayer?

_____

Read 1 Corinthians 10:12. Why should we make a deliberate commitment to stand with God?

_____

_____

Read Revelation 20:12. How will we be judged when we stand before God in the end?

_____

_____

_____

Read Mark 11:25. What should you be certain of before you stand praying before God?

_____

_____

_____

Read Romans 14:10. What should we not do? Why?

_____

_____

6. Your Commander Already Defeated the Enemy

Read Colossians 2:15. What did Jesus accomplish?

_____

_____

_____

Read Revelation 12:10-11. How has our accuser been defeated? How do we overcome him?

_____

_____

_____

Read Isaiah 59:19. How do we overcome the enemy's attack?

_____

_____

_____

Read 2 Thessalonians 3:3. What will the Lord do for us?

_____

_____

_____

7. Your Commander Is the Greatest Example of a Prayer Warrior

Read Matthew 6:9-13. Write out in your own words the prayer Jesus taught us. See also page 35 in the book.

_____

_____

_____

_____

_____

Read Romans 8:27,34. What does Jesus do for us?

_____

_____

_____

_____

WEEK THREE

Read Chapter 3:
"Recognize Who Your True Enemy Is"
in *Prayer Warrior*

1. The Truth About Who the Enemy Is

Read Isaiah 14:12-14. Read also page 39 in the book. Who was Lucifer? Whom did Lucifer want to be? What did he do and why?

_____

_____

_____

_____

Read Revelation 12:7-9. What was the result of Lucifer's battle for God's throne? Who did Lucifer become?

_____

_____

_____

_____

Read the following Scriptures or read pages 41-42 in the book. After each one, write out a short prayer asking God to protect you from the ploy of the enemy mentioned in those verses with regard to his name. (For example, after Matthew 4:3 you could pray, "Lord, help me to resist all temptation from the tempter...")

Matthew 4:3 _____

_____

_____

Matthew 6:13_____

_____

_____

John 14:30 _____

_____

_____

Ephesians 2:1-2_____

_____

_____

1 Peter 5:8 _____

_____

_____

2. The Truth About the Enemy's Lies

Read John 8:42-47. In this passage Jesus was talking to the Jews who did not believe Him. What did Jesus say about their father—who he is and what he does? (verses 42-44)

_____

_____

_____

Why did they not believe Him? Who hears God? (verses 45-47)

_____

_____

_____

Have there been times when you believed something you thought was true but it turned out to be a lie? Can you see where the source of that lie was the enemy? Explain.

_____

_____

_____

Has the enemy caused you to believe lies about yourself? Was there ever something you believed about yourself that you realized later was not true in light of God's Word? Explain.

_____

_____

_____

Write out a prayer asking God to help you identify the lies of the enemy and understand the truth of His Word.

_____

_____

3. The Enemy's First Deception

Read Revelation 12:9 and 20:2. Who is "the serpent of old"?

_____

_____

What happened to him? (12:9)

_____

_____

What *will* happen to him? (20:2)

_____

_____

Read Genesis 3:1-6. This is a story about "the serpent of old." In this passage the serpent first convinced Eve to doubt God's Word. What did Eve do as a result of believing the enemy's lies?

_____

_____

_____

Read Genesis 3:22-24. What did Adam and Eve lose as a result of her being *deceived* and him *choosing* to disobey God?

_____

_____

_____

_____

Write out a prayer asking God to help you identify the enemy when he comes disguised as something other than who he is. Ask for eyes to see the truth of God's Word and all that Jesus has done for you.

_____

_____

_____

_____

4. The Enemy Wants to Destroy Your Family

Read Exodus 12:23. Can you think of times when the enemy has tried to destroy your family—your marriage, your children, your family relationships, etc.? Explain one example that you have gone through or are going through now. Did you recognize it at the time as the enemy? What can God do?

_____

_____

_____

Write out a prayer asking God to show you any way in which the enemy is trying to—or *may* try to—destroy your family relationships, dynamics, or structure. Ask Him to reveal anything you need to see and show you how to resist the enemy and claim your family for the Lord.

_____

_____

_____

_____

5. The Enemy Wants Sin to Reign in Our Lives

Read 1 John 3:7-10. What is true of the person who continues to live in sin? (verses 7-8)

_____

_____

_____

Why did Jesus come? (verse 8)

_____

_____

What is true of someone who has been born again? (verse 9)

_____

_____

How can we distinguish between the children of God and the children of the devil? (verse 10)

_____

_____

_____

Read John 3:19-20. Why did people reject Jesus, the light of the world?

_____

_____

_____

Read Matthew 5:29-30. This passage is specifically talking about the sin of adultery, but what are we to do with whatever causes us to sin in our lives?

_____

_____

_____

Read the following Scriptures and write what they say about sin.

Matthew 5:19 _____

_____

_____

Ephesians 5:11-12 _____

_____

_____

James 1:15 _____

_____

_____

Write out a prayer asking God to reveal any sin in your life that needs to be confessed and repented of. If God shows you anything, confess it before Him and write it out below as a prayer to Him.

_____

_____

_____

6. Concentrate on the Goodness of God, Not the Work of the Enemy

Read John 10:10. Explain the difference between Jesus and the enemy in terms of what each one has planned for your life.

_____

_____

_____

Read John 10:11-14. What is the difference between the good shepherd—Jesus—and one who does not own the sheep? What happens when the enemy—the wolf—attacks?

_____

_____

_____

_____

What did Jesus do for you?

_____

_____

_____

Read John 15:15-16. What did Jesus do for you?

_____

_____

_____

7. The Enemy May Appear Strong to You, but Only God Is All-Powerful

Read John 10:28-30. Why are you safe from the enemy?

_____

_____

_____

_____

Read 1 John 4:4. Why are we guaranteed to overcome the enemy when we pray? How do we know God hears us?

_____

_____

_____

Read Ephesians 2:1-7. When we were dead in our sins, in what manner did we live? (verses 1-3)

_____

_____

_____

When we are made alive by the power of Jesus' death and resurrection, how do we now live? (verses 4-7)

_____

_____

_____

_____

Read the following Scriptures. What do they say about God's power?

1 Chronicles 29:11 _____

_____

_____

Matthew 6:13_____

_____

_____

1 Corinthians 6:14 _____

_____

_____

Ephesians 1:19-21 _____

_____

_____

Colossians 1:16_____

_____

_____

Write out a prayer asking God to help you always understand and remember how powerful He is so that you will never be intimidated by the enemy.

_____

_____

_____

_____

_____

8. People Who Reject God's Truth Will Be Given Over to a Spirit of Deception

Read 2 Thessalonians 2:9-12. Anyone who rejects God's truth will be given over to delusion. That is how the anti-Christ will deceive so many people. They will have already rejected God's truth and will fall easily into deception. They will have no spiritual discernment because they have already sold out the truth for a lie. What will be the result of their delusion?

_____

_____

_____

_____

_____

Read Romans 1:18-21. What does it say about people who reject God's truth? What happens to their mind and heart?

_____

_____

_____

_____

_____

Read 2 John 7. What are people called who do not confess that Jesus is the Son of God coming to earth?

_____

Write out a prayer asking God to help you receive His truth and clearly recognize the lies of the enemy so that you will never be deceived.

_____

_____

_____

_____

_____

Week Four

Read Chapter 4:

"Be Certain of Your Authority in Prayer"
in *Prayer Warrior*

1. You Have Authority Because You Have Jesus

Read the first two paragraphs on page 59 in the book. What is the most important thing you must be sure of as a prayer warrior? Complete the following sentences:

I must be sure of my _____

_____.

If I am not certain about that, the enemy will _____

_____

But the enemy will be shut down when I _____

_____ .

Read 2 Corinthians 13:3-5. Where does the power of God come from on our behalf? (verse 3)

_____

_____

How was Jesus resurrected? (verse 4)

_____

_____

Even though we are weak, how shall we live our lives? (verse 5)

_____

_____

Read 1 John 3:21-23. How do we have confidence toward God? (verse 21)

_____

_____

What happens when we keep His commandments? (verse 22)

_____

_____

What is His commandment? (verse 23)

_____

_____

Read Titus 2:13-14. What did Jesus do for us?

_____

_____

_____

2. You Have Authority Because of the Name of Jesus

Read the following Scriptures and answer the questions regarding the name of Jesus.

John 20:31. What can we have because of Jesus?

_____

_____

_____

1 Corinthians 6:9-11. What happened when we sinners received Jesus?

_____

_____

_____

Philippians 2:9-11. How powerful is the name of Jesus?

_____

_____

_____

Read Revelation 19:13,16. What are His names, and what do they indicate He is?

_____

_____

_____

Read Hebrews 13:15. What are we to do regarding His name?

_____

_____

_____

Read 2 Timothy 2:19. What is the seal of the solid foundation of God?

_____

_____

_____

Read Acts 4:12. Is there any other name by which we can be saved and why?

_____

_____

_____

3. You Have Authority Because Jesus Rescued You from the Tyranny of Evil

Read Revelation 3:5. What will Jesus do for you when you overcome the evil one and are called home to be with the Lord for eternity?

_____

_____

Read 1 Peter 3:22. This verse is about Jesus after His resurrection. Where did Jesus go, and what did He establish?

_____

_____

_____

Read Luke 10:17-19. What did Jesus give the 70 people He sent out?

_____

_____

_____

4. You Have Authority Because the Holy Spirit Is in You

Read Romans 8:9-11. According to these verses, if you have received Jesus, you are not in the flesh, but you are _____ , if the Spirit of God dwells _____ . If you do not have the Spirit of Christ—who is the Holy Spirit of God—then you are_____ . But if you have received Jesus, then the Holy Spirit, who raised Jesus from the dead, dwells in you. What will the Holy Spirit do for you?

_____

_____

When you are born again, you do not live in the flesh anymore because you have the Holy Spirit in you. That is how Jesus lives in you—through His Holy Spirit in you. And nothing can change that.

Read Ephesians 1:13. In light of this Scripture, what does believing in Jesus mean for you?

_____

_____

_____

Read Luke 9:1. What did Jesus give His disciples?

_____

_____

5. You Have Authority Because You Are Called

Read Luke 19:17. Because this man did what he was called to do, what did he receive?

_____

_____

_____

Read 1 Peter 2:9. What has God called you to do?

_____

_____

_____

Read 1 Peter 1:15. What has God called you to be and why?

_____

_____

_____

Read 2 Timothy 1:8-9. Who has called us and why?

_____

_____

_____

Read 1 Thessalonians 4:7. What did God call us to?

_____

_____

Read Romans 8:29-30. What is true of you and me and all who receive Jesus? What are we predestined to do?

_____

_____

_____

Read 2 Peter 1:10. What happens when we stand firm in our calling?

_____

_____

_____

6. You Have Authority Because You Are Forgiven

Read the following Scriptures and write down what we have because we are forgiven.

Acts 26:17-18 _____

_____

_____

Romans 4:7 _____

_____

_____

Ephesians 1:7-8 _____

_____

_____

Colossians 1:13-15 _____

_____

_____

Colossians 2:13 _____

_____

_____

1 John 1:9 _____

_____

_____

Week Five

Read Chapter 5:

"Condition Yourself to Be All You Can Be"
in *Prayer Warrior*

1. Spend Time with God in Prayer

In order to become all God made you to be—and do all He created you to do—you must be in close communication with Him. Spending time with the Lord in His Word, in worship, and in prayer feeds you so you can grow to maturity. You are renewed and strengthened every time you are in His presence. Jesus always spent time with His heavenly Father, and that is where He received power.

How would you describe your relationship with God? Is it close, intimate, distant, or strained? Do you gain strength when you are with Him? Do you long to be with Him in His Word, in prayer, and in worship? Do you have a need in your soul that can only be filled by His presence? Explain.

_____

_____

_____

_____

_____

Write out a prayer asking God to help you have the kind of relationship with Him you want to have. Be specific.

_____

_____

_____

_____

_____

Read Psalm 37:4-11. What does it say about people who delight, trust, and rest in the Lord—which is actually what praying accomplishes?

_____

_____

_____

_____

_____

Read 1 Thessalonians 5:16-17. What is the will of God concerning you? Do you feel you are in God's will with regard to these things? Write out your answer as a prayer asking God to help you always be in His perfect will, specifically mentioning these things.

_____

_____

_____

_____

2. Live in a Way That Pleases God

What are some of the things that please God? (See pages 77-81 in the book.)

_____

_____

_____

_____

_____

Read Hebrews 2:1. See also page 78 in the book, the first three paragraphs. What must we do to keep from drifting away from the things of God? Write your answer out as a prayer asking God to help you do exactly that.

_____

_____

_____

_____

_____

Read John 14:15,23. What pleases God? Why are reading, studying, and doing the Word of God so important?

_____

_____

_____

_____

Read page 78 in the book, the last full paragraph. How do we show our love for God? What happens when we do that?

_____

_____

_____

_____

Read 1 John 3:8-9. When someone continues to live in sin, what is true about them? (verse 8)

_____

_____

_____

What is true of those who do not sin? (verse 9)

_____

_____

_____

Read Romans 8:8. How do we please God?

_____

_____

Write out a prayer asking God to show you anything in your heart that does not please Him.

_____

_____

_____

3. Acknowledge God's Call to Holiness

Read 1 Peter 1:13-16. How are we to be holy?

_____

_____

_____

_____

We can stop doing, saying, or thinking things that are not holy, but we cannot make ourselves be holy. Only by receiving Jesus and His Holy Spirit to dwell in us—and allowing the Spirit of Christ (Romans 8:9) to wash us—are we made holy. This flow of living water does not run out or run dry.

Read John 4:7-14. What did Jesus say to the woman about the fountain of water that He gives us? (verses 13-14)

_____

_____

_____

_____

Read John 7:38. Where do the rivers of living water in us come from and why?

_____

_____

When you receive Jesus, He gives you a flow of living water in you, who is the Holy Spirit. Because of Him you will never thirst again. But in order to receive the full flow of this living water, you must thirst for a fresh flow of it every day. The Holy Spirit gives us all that He is—even His holiness—but we have to be open to all He has for us by welcoming Him to work in us and change us into the image of Christ. Write out a prayer asking God to do all of that in you.

_____

_____

_____

_____

_____

4. Get Rid of Anything in Your Life That Is Not Glorifying to God

Read James 4:8. What does God want us to do?

_____

_____

Read Ephesians 4:30. What does God want us to never do?

_____

_____

Read Galatians 5:17. What opposes the Holy Spirit?

_____

_____

_____

Read Deuteronomy 5:33. Why does God want us to separate ourselves from sin?

_____

_____

Read Psalm 66:18. What happens when we don't separate ourselves from sin?

_____

_____

_____

Read 1 John 1:8-9. What does it mean if we think we would never sin? (verse 8)

_____

_____

_____

What should we do when we detect sin in our lives, and what will happen as a result of doing that? (verse 9)

_____

_____

_____

Read Deuteronomy 6:13-15. What does God want His people to do and *not* do?

_____

_____

A life of holiness is not possible without being separate from the world. But that does not mean we are isolated from the world. We are still *in* it, but we are not *of* it. That means we don't buy in to the godless or anti-Christ spirit in the world. Living a holy life means we separate ourselves from all that is not holy. Write out a prayer asking God to help you separate yourself from all godlessness and be a light in the world.

_____

_____

_____

_____

_____

5. Refuse All Pride

Read 1 John 2:16. What does this verse say about pride?

_____

_____

Read Proverbs 16:18. What happens as a result of pride?

_____

_____

Read Obadiah. What does pride do to us?

_____

_____

_____

Write out a prayer asking God to reveal to you any pride in your heart. If He shows you something, write out a confession of your recognition and repentance to God and ask Him to deliver you from pride and all the consequences of it.

_____

_____

_____

_____

_____

6. Fulfill God's Command to Love Others

Read 1 John 3:10. What does it reveal about us when we don't have love for others?

_____

_____

_____

Read 1 John 3:14-15. What do these verses say about us if we don't have love for our brothers and sisters in Christ?

_____

_____

_____

Read Romans 5:5. How can we have love for others?

_____

_____

Read Galatians 5:6. What is important in our lives?

_____

_____

Read Ephesians 5:2. What are we to do and why?

_____

_____

_____

Read 1 Corinthians 13:1-3. What is the result of not having love in our hearts?

_____

_____

_____

Read Matthew 22:36-37. What is the greatest commandment?

_____

_____

_____

7. Don't Be Careless with Your Body

Read Hebrews 10:22. What does God want us to do?

_____

_____

_____

Read 1 Thessalonians 4:3-8. What does God *not* want us to do with our body and why?

_____

_____

_____

Read 1 Corinthians 3:16-17. What happens if we defile our bodies?

_____

_____

_____

Read 1 Corinthians 6:19-20. What is the main reason we need to care for and purify our body?

_____

_____

Read Hebrews 4:10-11. What does God want you to do for your body? Write out your answer as a prayer asking God to help you do that.

_____

_____

Read Romans 12:1. What are you supposed to do with your body?

_____

_____

8. Separate Yourself from the Ungodly

Read 2 Corinthians 6:17-18. Why do we need to be separate?

_____

_____

_____

_____

_____

Read Romans 12:2. What should you do and why?

_____

_____

_____

Read Philippians 2:14-16. How can we be separate from those who are ungodly?

_____

_____

_____

Read Psalm 1:1-3. What is the reward for you when you do not walk with the ungodly?

_____

_____

_____

_____

Read 2 Corinthians 6:14. Why are you not to spend too much time with ungodly people and be drawn into anything that compromises your walk with God?

_____

_____

_____

_____

Read Ephesians 5:11. What does this verse say to do? Why do you think this is especially important to do as a prayer warrior?

_____

_____

_____

9. Don't Dwell on What You Are Not

Read Romans 8:16-17. Who does God say you are?

_____

_____

_____

_____

Read John 1:12. What did Jesus do for you?

_____

_____

_____

Read 1 John 3:1-2. What is promised for you?

_____

_____

_____

What negative things has the enemy, or a misguided person, told you about yourself that you know is not true or you want to believe is not true? Write out your answer as a prayer to God. (For example, "Lord, I have been believing about myself that...") Ask God to show you the truth about yourself. Ask Him to help you distinguish the truth from the enemy's lies so you can become all He created you to be.

_____

_____

_____

_____

10. Walk in a Way to Produce the Fruit of the Spirit

Read Galatians 5:22-23. The Bible lists nine different things as "the fruit of the Spirit." Write down each one and put a number beside it on a scale of 1 to 10—with 10 being the highest—how well you think you manifest that fruit in your life.

_____

_____

_____

_____

_____

Read Ephesians 5:8-10. How are we to walk in order to produce the fruit of the Spirit?

_____

_____

_____

Read Galatians 5:24-25. How are we to walk in the Spirit?

_____

_____

_____

When you are led by the Spirit in all you do, you will walk in the Spirit. In light of the Scriptures above, write out a prayer asking God to help you walk in a way that produces the fruit of the Spirit.

_____

_____

_____

_____

_____

11. Be Renewed in Your Mind

Read Ephesians 4:23-24. What are we supposed to do?

_____

_____

_____

Read Ephesians 4:17-19. How should we never walk?

_____

_____

_____

Read Romans 12:2. How can we be transformed, and what happens as a result?

_____

_____

_____

Read 1 Corinthians 2:16. What do we have as believers, and how do we benefit from that?

_____

_____

_____

Read Hebrews 8:10. What does God want to do in us?

_____

_____

_____

Read 2 Timothy 1:7. What has God not given to you? What *has* He given you?

_____

_____

_____

Read 2 Corinthians 10:5. What are you supposed to do with your mind?

_____

_____

_____

12. Be Forgiving at All Times

Read Luke 7:47. Do you feel you have been forgiven a little or a lot? Does that seem to correspond to your love for Him?

_____

_____

_____

_____

Read Mark 11:25-26. What happens when we don't forgive others?

_____

_____

_____

Read Ephesians 4:32. What are you always supposed to do?

_____

_____

_____

Read Colossians 3:12-13. As God's child, what should you do?

_____

_____

_____

Read Matthew 6:14-15. What happens if you don't forgive others?

_____

_____

_____

Write out a prayer asking God to show you any place in you where there is unforgiveness. If you know of any, confess it to God and ask to be forgiven and set free of it.

_____

_____

_____

_____

_____

13. Watch What You Say

Read 1 Peter 3:10-12. What must we do in order to have a good life? What are the consequences if we don't do that?

_____

_____

_____

_____

Read Matthew 12:34. What influences the words we speak?

_____

_____

_____

Read 1 Peter 3:15-16. What are we to say and when? Why are we to do that?

_____

_____

_____

Read the following Scriptures and next to each one write what it says about the words we say.

Proverbs 16:23 _____

_____

Proverbs 29:11 _____

_____

Proverbs 29:20 _____

_____

Ecclesiastes 5:3 _____

_____

Ecclesiastes 10:12 _____

_____

Matthew 12:36_____

_____

Matthew 15:18 _____

_____

Ephesians 4:25 _____

_____

Proverbs 15:23 _____

_____

Week Six

Read Chapter 6:
"Put On Your Protective Armor Each Morning"
in *Prayer Warrior*

1. Gird Your Waist with the Truth

Read Ephesians 6:10-11. Why must we put on the whole armor of God?

_____

_____

_____

Read Ephesians 6:12. What do we struggle against? What do we *not* struggle against?

_____

_____

_____

Read 1 John 5:19. Who sways us away from the truth? Who lives under his lies and deception?

_____

_____

_____

Read John 8:31-32. How do we become disciples of Jesus? What makes us free?

_____

_____

_____

Read Colossians 2:15. What did Jesus do with regard to evil?

_____

_____

_____

Write out a prayer asking God to help you live only in His truth and never accept lies for truth.

_____

_____

_____

_____

_____

2. Put On the Breastplate of Righteousness

Read 2 Corinthians 6:3-7. In verse 7, it says Paul conducts his life and ministry by what?

_____

_____

_____

Read 2 Corinthians 5:21. How have we become the righteousness of God?

_____

_____

_____

Read Romans 6:13. How are we to present ourselves before God?

_____

_____

_____

Read Romans 14:17. How do we live in the kingdom of God?

_____

_____

_____

Read Isaiah 61:10. Why should we praise God?

_____

_____

_____

3. Shoe Your Feet with the Preparation of the Gospel of Peace

When we stand on the good news and truth of Jesus in our lives, it makes us sure-footed and secure, and that brings us peace.

Read Ephesians 2:14. Where does our peace come from?

_____

_____

_____

_____

Read Philippians 4:7. What does the peace of God do for you?

_____

_____

_____

_____

Read Colossians 3:15. What are we supposed to do?

_____

_____

_____

_____

Write out a prayer asking God to help you stand secure in all Jesus has done for you and thanking Him for His peace that is beyond comprehension.

_____

_____

_____

_____

4. Take the Shield of Faith

Read the following Scriptures, and in your own words write out what each one means to you in regard to your faith.

Genesis 15:1 _____

_____

_____

Psalm 56:11 _____

_____

_____

Mark 5:36 _____

_____

_____

Mark 9:23 _____

_____

_____

Write out a prayer asking God to give you faith so strong it takes away fear and becomes a shield to you from the enemy.

_____

_____

_____

_____

5. Take the Helmet of Salvation

What does it mean to our lives that we have been saved by the
Lord Jesus? See page 104 in the book, the last paragraph.

_____

_____

_____

_____

Read Psalm 140:7. What does God do when you are in a battle with the enemy?

_____

_____

_____

Read 1 Thessalonians 5:8. What are we to do every day?

_____

_____

_____

6. Take the Sword of the Spirit, Which Is the Word of God

Read Hebrews 4:12. Describe the Word of God as told here.

_____

_____

_____

Read 2 Timothy 3:16-17. Why do we need to have the Word of God in our mind, memory, and heart?

_____

_____

_____

7. Pray Always with All Prayer and Supplication in the Spirit

Read Philippians 4:6. What are we to do? Write out your answer as a prayer asking God to help you do it.

_____

_____

_____

Read 1 Thessalonians 5:17. How are we to pray? Write out your answer as a prayer asking God to help you do it.

_____

_____

_____

Read Colossians 4:2. What are we to do? Write out your answer as a prayer asking God to help you do it.

_____

_____

_____

_____

Read Mark 13:33. What are we to do and why?

_____

_____

_____

Read 1 John 5:14. What are we to pray and why?

_____

_____

_____

Read John 15:7. What are we to do and why?

_____

_____

_____

Read Luke 11:9-10. What are we to do? What happens when we do that?

_____

_____

_____

8. Be Watchful to the End

Read Luke 18:1. What are we to *not* do as we pray?

_____

_____

Read Song of Solomon 3:8. What does this Scripture tell you about a warrior's readiness?

_____

_____

_____

Read Luke 21:36. Why should we be watchful?

_____

_____

_____

Read 1 Corinthians 16:13. What are we to do?

_____

_____

_____

Read Ephesians 6:18. How are we to pray?

_____

_____

_____

Read 2 Timothy 4:5. What are we to do?

_____

_____

_____

Read 1 Peter 4:7. What are we to do and why?

_____

_____

_____

Read Luke 21:36. What are we to do and why?

_____

_____

_____

Read Luke 12:37. Why were the servants blessed, and what was their reward?

_____

_____

_____

Read Mark 13:37. What did Jesus say to us all?

_____

_____

_____

Week Seven

Read Chapter 7:
"Become Skilled with Your Spiritual Weapons"
in *Prayer Warrior*

1. The Sword of the Spirit Is Our Main Weapon Against the Enemy

Read Revelation 1:10-18. The apostle John was "in the Spirit on the Lord's Day" and was given this prophecy of what is and what is to come. The voice he heard was that of Jesus.

How did Jesus describe Himself? (verses 10-11)

_____

_____

_____

_____

How did John describe Jesus? (verse12-16)

_____

_____

_____

_____

What did Jesus have coming out of His mouth? (verse 16)

_____

_____

What did Jesus say to John? (verses 17-18)

_____

_____

Read John 1:1-14. What does the passage say about the Word? (verses 1-2)

_____

_____

What did Jesus accomplish? (verse 3)

_____

_____

_____

What is in Jesus? Who does not comprehend it? (verses 4-5)

_____

_____

What does John say about who Jesus was and is? (verses 9-11)

_____

_____

_____

What does Jesus give to those who receive Him? (verses 12-13)

_____

_____

_____

What is Jesus called, and how is He depicted? (verse 14)

_____

_____

_____

Read Ephesians 6:17. What is the sword of the Spirit?

_____

_____

_____

Read Hebrews 4:12. What does the Word of God do?

_____

_____

_____

Putting everything together that you have just read, why do you think the Word of God is a powerful and crucial weapon in the battle against our enemy?

_____

_____

_____

Read Luke 4:1-13. This passage is about Jesus being tempted three times by the devil in the wilderness. A big part of the enemy's attack on us is through temptation to disobey God's will, ways, and Word. What did Jesus use as His weapon against the enemy? (verses 4,8,12)

_____

_____

_____

_____

_____

In light of the Scriptures above, what can you conclude is your greatest weapon against the enemy and why?

_____

_____

_____

_____

Write out a prayer asking God to help you become skilled at using the Word against the enemy when he attacks you.

_____

_____

_____

_____

_____

2. Worship Is a Powerful Weapon Against the Enemy

Read John 4:23-24. What did Jesus say the Father wants from us?

_____

_____

_____

Read 2 Corinthians 3:17-18. What happens when we worship God? See also the last full paragraph on page 117 in the book and the following paragraph, which ends on page 118.

_____

_____

_____

_____

Read Philippians 4:4. How often should we praise God?

_____

_____

_____

_____

Read Psalm 22:3. Where does God's presence become enthroned or dwell?

_____

_____

_____

When we worship God, His presence comes to dwell with us. Why do you think the enemy doesn't want to be around us when we worship God? See page 118, the second and third paragraphs. How is this a good thing with regard to spiritual warfare?

_____

_____

_____

_____

Read Hebrews 13:15. How often should we worship and praise God?

_____

_____

_____

Read the second and third paragraphs on page 118 in the book. How should we react to an enemy attack?

_____

_____

_____

Write out a prayer of praise and worship to God that you can pray anytime—especially when the enemy attacks. Include these Scriptures above or ones mentioned in the book, or any others you find in your Bible. This prayer can become so much a part of your worship that it will naturally be your first response to an enemy attack.

_____

_____

_____

_____

_____

3. God's Grace Is a Weapon Against the Enemy

Read Ephesians 2:8. Read also the first paragraph on page 119 in the book under the subtitle above. What is grace, and what is true of God's grace?

_____

_____

_____

_____

Read Hebrews 4:16. What can we do in times of trouble and need?

_____

_____

_____

Read James 4:6. Whom does God resist and to whom does He extend grace?

_____

_____

_____

Read 1 Peter 1:13. Where are we to put our hope?

_____

_____

_____

Read about Zerubbabel learning to speak grace to an impossible situation on pages 119-120 in the book under the heading "God's Grace Is a Weapon Against the Enemy." How would the temple be rebuilt in the midst of satanic opposition?

_____

_____

_____

_____

What can we learn from that when we face enemy opposition?

_____

_____

_____

_____

Why can't the enemy have power when we speak grace to an impossible situation in our lives?

_____

_____

_____

_____

Is there a situation in your life that seems impossible? Write down what that situation is. Below that, write out a prayer speaking "grace" to that mountain (that impossible situation) and thank God He can level it to become a flat plain.

My impossible situation:_____

_____

_____

_____

_____

My prayer of grace for that situation: _____

_____

_____

_____

_____

4. Fasting with Prayer Is a Weapon Against the Enemy

Read Isaiah 58:6-14. This is the main passage in the Bible that describes the kind of fast God wants from us. (The previous verses 1-5 describe the kind of fast that God does *not* want.) What can fasting and prayer accomplish against the enemy? (verse 6)

_____

_____

_____

_____

What does God want us to do as our fasting makes us sensitive to His commands? (verse 7)

_____

_____

_____

_____

_____

What will happen when we obey God and fast? (verse 8)

_____

_____

_____

_____

_____

What will be God's reward for you when you fast? (verse 9)

_____

_____

_____

_____

_____

What will happen when we extend ourselves to others? (verses 10-11)

_____

_____

_____

_____

_____

Have you ever fasted?

_____

How hard was fasting for you?

_____

How often do you fast?

_____

Can you think of a situation in your life that needs break-through? Are you willing to fast for that? Describe.

_____

_____

_____

_____

How much do you think you can do as a fast? One meal, two meals, three meals? Twenty-four hours, thirty-six hours, or longer? Write out your answer as a prayer, asking God to show you what He wants you to do regarding fasting and asking Him to help you take the steps you believe you can do. For example, "Lord, show me if I should fast and pray for two meals on Monday in order to loose the bonds of wickedness in this situation that is so troubling to me." Then, as you follow through on the fast, write down in your journal what you experienced during or after the fast regarding your relationship with the Lord—how He spoke to your heart—and what happened in the situation you prayed about.

_____

_____

_____

_____

5. Faith Is a Shield *and* a Weapon Against the Enemy

Read Hebrews 11:6. What must we believe in order to please God?

_____

_____

_____

Read James 1:6-7. How are we to pray and why?

_____

_____

_____

Read Hebrews 10:38. How are we to live? What happens when we don't live that way?

_____

_____

_____

Read Hebrews 11:1-11. Complete the sentences started below.

Faith is (verse 1):_____

_____

By faith we (verse 3):_____

_____

By faith Abel offered (verse 4): _____

_____

By faith Enoch was (verse 5): _____

_____

_____

By faith Noah (verse 7): _____

_____

_____

By faith Abraham (verses 8-10): _____

_____

_____

By faith Sarah (verse 11): _____

_____

_____

From these Scriptures, how do you think that having faith in God and His Word becomes a weapon against the enemy?

_____

_____

_____

_____

Write out a prayer asking God to help you have strong faith the way these great people of Bible times did.

_____

_____

_____

_____

_____

6. Prayer Is Always a Powerful Weapon Against the Enemy

Prayer is the battle itself. The battle is waged in prayer. What do the following Scriptures say about how we are to pray?

Mark 13:33 _____

_____

_____

Mark 14:38 _____

_____

_____

Luke 11:2 _____

_____

_____

Luke 18:1 _____

_____

_____

Romans 8:26 _____

_____

_____

1 Thessalonians 5:17 _____

_____

_____

1 Timothy 2:8 _____

_____

_____

James 5:13 _____

_____

_____

One of the most important things Jesus prayed for was for His Father God's will to be done. How does our praying for God's will serve as a weapon against the enemy?

_____

_____

_____

Write out a prayer asking God to help you pray in power and according to His will. Include any of the above Scriptures that you want.

_____

_____

_____

_____

_____

WEEK EIGHT

Read Chapter 8:

"Engage in the War Knowing Time Is Short"
in *Prayer Warrior*

1. Engage Because You Don't Know All That Your Prayers May Accomplish

This chapter is about your commitment to serve your Lord and Savior in spiritual warfare because the time of the Lord's return grows closer, and that means the enemy knows he has but a short time left and is pulling out all the stops. Not that he was ever restraining himself, but the exponential increase of evil in the world cannot be hidden or ignored. We cannot sit on the sidelines watching as if our lives and the lives of our family members and people we love will not be affected by this.

With regard to being a prayer warrior, what does "engage in the war" mean? See page 130 in the book, the first two paragraphs.

_____

_____

_____

_____

_____

Why do we need more prayer warriors actively engaged in prayer? See page 130, the fourth paragraph.

_____

_____

_____

Read Revelation 5:8. What is in the golden bowls of incense that are presented to Jesus? What does that say about your prayers?

_____

_____

_____

Read Revelation 12:7-11. Who fights in the war in heaven? (verse 7)

_____

_____

_____

Who is the great dragon, and what happened to him? (verse 9)

_____

_____

_____

What came against the enemy, and what was the result? (verse 10)

_____

_____

_____

How did the believers overcome the enemy? (verse 11)

_____

_____

_____

Write out briefly what you would like to see your prayers accomplish. Write it out as a commitment prayer to God. (For example, "Lord, I commit my life to You in prayer. Lead me as to how to pray. Tell me what to pray at all times. What I would like to see happen as a result of my prayers is…")

_____

_____

_____

_____

_____

Read 2 Corinthians 9:6-7. What do these verses mean to you with regard to the time you spend in prayer? Do you believe God will accomplish more through you if you pray more?

_____

_____

_____

_____

Whom or what have you been praying for, or *wanting* to pray for, lately? For example, my prayer group and I have a burden on our hearts to pray for boys and girls and women who have been kidnapped and are still alive. We pray they will be able to escape their captors. We started doing this before the release of the women in recent years who have been able to escape. We believe there are many more out there. We pray with specific names of those we know of who have not yet been found, but we also pray generally as well because God knows their names even though we don't, and He knows exactly where they are. Write out a prayer below asking God to show you who He wants you to pray for right now. When He brings someone to mind, ask the Holy Spirit to lead you as to how to pray for that person or those people specifically.

_____

_____

_____

_____

_____

2. Engage Because You Serve God

Read Deuteronomy 6:13. What are we to do?

_____

_____

_____

Read Matthew 20:26-28. If we want to do something great for the Lord, what should we do? Why?

_____

_____

Read Colossians 3:23-24. What are we to do and why?

_____

_____

_____

_____

_____

We serve God because we love Him. When we show our love for God by our service to Him in prayer, the commitment to pray seems easy. Read page 134 in the book, the second full paragraph. What are you doing when you are praying as God's prayer warrior?

_____

_____

_____

_____

Write out a prayer telling God you want to serve Him as His prayer warrior in every way that pleases Him.

_____

_____

_____

_____

3. Engage Because You Know the Time Is Short

Read Romans 13:12. See also page 137 in the book, the first paragraph. What is the "armor of light"?

_____

_____

_____

Read Revelation 12:12. Because the devil knows his time is limited, he is trying to draw as many people into hell with him as he can. What do you think we prayer warriors do to restrict that? As his rage grows against us, what do you believe should grow in us as prayer warriors at the same time?

_____

_____

_____

_____

Read Revelation 20:1-3. What is Satan's future?

_____

_____

_____

_____

All of this points to the increase of satanic work on earth. In response to that, what do you think we as prayer warriors should do? Write out your answer as a prayer asking God to help us do that.

_____

_____

_____

_____

_____

4. Engage Because You Are Engaged

If you find someone you want to spend the rest of your life with, how much time do you want to spend with him (or her)? How close do you want your relationship to be? How much do you want to please him (or her)?

_____

_____

_____

_____

How would you describe your relationship with God? Do you feel committed to Him? Do you want to serve Him? If so, how committed are you? Do you feel you have engaged with Him in that you read the Word, pray, and spend time in worship with the intent of drawing closer to Him and knowing Him better? Explain.

_____

_____

_____

_____

Write out a prayer of commitment to the Lord and ask Him to help you become so engaged with Him that engaging in prayer in the war against evil is an easy decision. Tell Him that to not engage as a prayer warrior in the war against Him and all who believe in Him would be unthinkable.

_____

_____

_____

_____

_____

Read the following Scriptures on prayer. Beside each one describe what is being prayed for.

Mark 14:38 _____

_____

Luke 21:36 _____

_____

2 Corinthians 13:9 _____

_____

Colossians 1:9_____

_____

2 Thessalonians 1:11 _____

_____

James 5:13 _____

_____

James 5:14 _____

_____

James 5:18 _____

_____

3 John 2 _____

_____

Week Nine

Read Chapter 9:

"Identify the Immediate Battlefield"
in *Prayer Warrior*

1. The Battlefield in the Fight for Your Clarity of Mind

The battlefield in spiritual warfare is wherever you are praying. That's because *you* are choosing the battlefield. However, if you are not praying, the enemy will choose the battlefield *for* you. It will be wherever he decides to attack you or someone you care about. If we don't advance *God's* kingdom in prayer, the enemy will advance *his*. The enemy's kingdom is the godless and anti-Christ worldview that is far too much in control in this world. But we can change that. Read the following Scriptures. After each one write down how the enemy is described and what it says about him.

John 12:31 _____

_____

_____

John 16:8-11_____

_____

_____

Ephesians 2:1-2_____

_____

_____

Read Matthew 11:12. Also read page 143 in the book, the last two lines to the end of that paragraph on page 144. To whom has God given the responsibility for advancing His kingdom?

_____

_____

God gives us His kingdom, but what do we still have to do?

_____

_____

What does it mean that we have to get violent in order to take the kingdom? Who is opposing us? What is the battle?

_____

_____

_____

_____

What are some of the battlefields that the enemy has brought to you? Describe. (For example, "The enemy has brought the battlefield to me in the area of my finances, my work, my health, and/or my relationships...")

_____

_____

_____

_____

_____

Of the battlefields you listed above, did you know at the time they were battlefields where the enemy was attacking you, or did you think they were just things that happened to you, or did you blame yourself for what was happening? Could you have benefited from your own powerful prayer if you had prayed in advance of, or during, that attack? Explain.

_____

_____

_____

_____

_____

Read John 8:44. The enemy will always try to attack us in our mind. He is the master of deception and the father of lies. Read also page 145 in the book, the second, third, and fourth paragraphs, and answer the questions below.

Why does the enemy speak lies to your mind?

_____

_____

_____

_____

_____

Why do you think your mind is one of the enemy's favorite places to attack you?

_____

_____

_____

_____

Read 2 Corinthians 10:4-5. Describe your weapons. What should you do to stand against the attack of the enemy in the area of your mind?

_____

_____

_____

_____

Does the enemy ever attack you in your mind? Do you ever have negative thoughts that play over and over? Write out your answer as a prayer to God. Tell Him the specific thoughts you have struggled with and ask Him to take these thoughts away and fill your mind with His truth. (For example, "Lord, I have negative thoughts about myself and my life, and I feel like a failure much of the time...")

_____

_____

_____

_____

_____

Read Philippians 2:5. What should you do?

_____

_____

_____

Read 1 Corinthians 2:16. What should be in your mind? Write your answer out as a prayer asking God for a fresh infilling of His Spirit every day so that your mind is filled with thoughts of Him and His truth.

_____

_____

_____

Read Ephesians 4:22-24. What must you do? Write your answer out as a prayer to God. (For example, "Lord, I pray You would help me to put away sinful conduct and any way I have tried to live without You...")

_____

_____

_____

Read 1 Corinthians 14:33. Who do you think is the author of confusion?

_____

_____

_____

_____

Where does your peace come from?

_____

_____

Read Isaiah 26:3. How do we live in perfect peace?

_____

_____

Read Philippians 4:8. Write out a prayer asking God to show you if you have accepted any lies of the enemy as truth and to set you free of them. Then ask Him to help you think about the specific things mentioned in this verse.

_____

_____

_____

_____

2. The Battlefield in the Fight for Your Children's Lives

Even if you don't have children in your life right now, the principles here can also apply to yourself and the attacks on your life. Perhaps your own parents did not know how to intercede for your life and the enemy was able to lead you away from God's best for you. If so, write out a prayer of protection for yourself now and let this open your eyes to the devil's tactics for young and defenseless people—people who are not being covered by prayer warrior parents.

_____

_____

_____

_____

_____

Read 1 Peter 5:8. In light of this Scripture, what can you conclude about the enemy's intention for your children?

_____

_____

_____

Read Revelation 12:4. In light of this Scripture, what does the enemy like to do with children who will be raised up to serve God? This verse is talking about Jesus, but we can see what the enemy's intention is for any child who threatens his rule in the world.

_____

_____

_____

Read Matthew 7:11. In light of this Scripture, what can you conclude about how God will respond to your prayers for your children?

_____

_____

_____

_____

Read Psalm 103:17-18. What is the promise of God to us concerning our children and grandchildren if we live His way and go to battle in prayer for them?

_____

_____

_____

_____

Read Lamentations 2:19. What are we to do for our children?

_____

_____

_____

Read Proverbs 11:21. What is true of the children of believers?

_____

_____

_____

Read Psalm 18:48 and Isaiah 43:2. Write out these Scriptures as a prayer for your children. (For example, "Lord, I lift my daughter to you and pray You will deliver her from the enemy and be with her...")

_____

_____

_____

_____

Read Deuteronomy 30:19. What is the promise for our children if we choose to live God's way? Write out your answer as a prayer asking God to help you live His way so that your children will be blessed.

_____

_____

_____

_____

Read Isaiah 30:1. What does this Scripture say about children who rebel? What do rebellious children do?

_____

_____

_____

Read 1 Samuel 15:23. What are rebellion and stubbornness like? What can happen when children rebel and are not corrected?

_____

_____

_____

Read Isaiah 1:19-20. Pride and rebellion in a child are illustrated when a child says, "I want what *I* want when *I* want it." In light of these verses, what happens to those who are rebellious? What happens if they are obedient?

_____

_____

_____

Read Psalm 107:10-12. What happened to those who were rebellious?

_____

_____

_____

_____

Read Nehemiah 9:26-27. What happened to those who were rebellious?

_____

_____

_____

_____

The enemy wants our children to serve him. A door is opened to them when they are rebellious and we as parents or authority figures in their lives allow them to continue on that path without consequences or confrontation or prayer. We need to go to battle against the enemy by declaring that our children belong to God, and we will not tolerate anything bordering on witchcraft—as rebellion is described in the Bible—to become a stronghold in their lives. Write out a prayer for your child or children—or children you know of—resisting the enemy on their behalf. Ask God to break any stronghold of the enemy, especially a rebellious nature, that the enemy has set up for their downfall.

_____

_____

_____

_____

_____

3. The Battlefield in the Fight for Your Marriage

The key here is fighting *for* your marriage, not fighting *in* your marriage. It is recognizing who your true enemy is, and it is not your spouse—that is, unless he or she has gone completely over to the dark side. The enemy will attack us in the area of marriage by telling us that we deserve better than this. And if one or both parties become selfish, rude, and cruel, it will play right into the enemy's hand. Have you ever sensed the enemy's attack in a marriage, whether it was your marriage, or the marriage of someone you know well, or your parents' marriage? In what way did you recognize the hand of the enemy?

_____

_____

_____

_____

_____

Read Matthew 22:37-39. In light of these verses, what should our two top priorities be in a marriage?

_____

_____

_____

What do you think violating those top two priorities will do as far as allowing your marriage to become a battlefield?

_____

_____

_____

_____

Read 1 Peter 5:5. In light of this Scripture, how is a married couple supposed to act toward one another?

_____

_____

_____

_____

Read 1 Timothy 3:6. What can being puffed up with pride cause us to do? When a person acts like the devil, what will the results be?

_____

_____

_____

Have you ever experienced pride in your marriage? (Or in a relationship, if you have never been married?) How does pride affect the relationship?

_____

_____

_____

Write out a prayer asking God to take away all pride in you and your spouse so that the enemy has no point of entry into your marriage relationship.

Read 1 Thessalonians 5:15. In light of this Scripture, what can damage a marriage? What should a husband and wife do instead?

Read 1 Peter 3:8-12. Write out these verses as a prayer for your marriage. (For example, "Lord, I pray You will help my husband [wife] and me to be of one mind and not be at odds. Give us a heart of compassion for each other…") If you are not married, write these verses out as a prayer for your future marriage or for someone else's marriage relationship you know is being attacked by the enemy.

Write out a prayer listing some ways the enemy has attacked your marriage in the past, or is attacking it right now, and how you want God to change that. If you are not married, write this prayer for someone who is married.

_____

_____

_____

_____

_____

Write out a prayer inviting God and all He is into your marriage relationship. Ask Him to root out anything in either of you that gives the enemy reason to believe he has something in one or both of you that allows him to drive a wedge between you. If you are not married, write this prayer for someone who is.

_____

_____

_____

_____

_____

Week Ten

Read Chapter 10:

"Follow His Orders to Resist the Enemy"
in *Prayer Warrior*

1. Resist the Enemy by Rejecting Pride

A lot has been said about pride in this book because it is the defining characteristic of the enemy. Resisting pride in ourselves is one of the ways we resist the enemy in our lives. Read James 4:6. What does God do regarding prideful people?

_____

_____

What does God do regarding people who are humble?

_____

_____

Read page 159 in the book, the last two paragraphs. What are the three things that separate us from God?

_____

_____

_____

What can put a stop to all that in our lives?

_____

_____

Read James 4:7-10 and answer the following questions.

What can we do to resist the devil? And what will he do in response? (verse 7)

_____

_____

_____

What does it mean to submit to God? (verses 8-9)

_____

_____

_____

What are we to do before God? What will He do in response? (verse 10)

_____

_____

_____

Write out verses 7-10 as a prayer asking God to help you do these things. (For example, "Lord, help me to submit to You in every way so that I can successfully resist the devil, knowing he will flee from me. Help me to…")

_____

_____

_____

_____

_____

Read page 160 in the book, the third and fourth paragraphs. Why do we have to submit our weaknesses—the areas in which we can be most tempted—to God? What happens when we do that?

_____

_____

_____

_____

What are the weakest areas of your personality that you realize must be submitted to God so He can help you watch over them? Write out your answer as a prayer to God submitting that weakness to Him and telling Him you depend on Him to help you stay strong. (For example, "Lord, my weakness is spending too much…being critical…seeking attention…being impatient…speaking sharply…")

_____

_____

_____

_____

Read Psalm 10:17 and Isaiah 57:15. What does God do for the humble?

_____

_____

_____

_____

Read page 162 in the book, the second and third paragraphs. What are two of the things God does for us when we are humble? Why do you think these things are especially important to us as prayer warriors?

_____

_____

_____

_____

_____

2. Resist the Enemy by Refusing Fear

Read 2 Timothy 1:7. What has God given you?

_____

_____

What has God definitely not given you?

_____

_____

_____

This doesn't mean that if you are ever afraid then God is not ruling in your life. There are many reasons to be afraid in this world. But we must not be continually ruled by fear and give place to a *spirit of fear*. Where do you believe a spirit of fear comes from?

_____

_____

_____

Part of resisting the enemy is refusing to act like him. We need godly wisdom in order to do that. This kind of wisdom brings understanding and humility, as opposed to what is perceived as worldly wisdom that promotes pride.

Read James 3:16-18. What comes as a result of envy and self-seeking? (verse 16)

_____

_____

_____

What comes as a result of having godly wisdom? (verse 17)

_____

_____

_____

What do those who make peace produce? (verse 18)

_____

_____

_____

_____

Write out a prayer asking God to give you wisdom and peace so that you will always be able to resist the fear the enemy and the world want to put on you.

_____

_____

_____

_____

_____

_____

3. Resist the Enemy by Praying for Miracles

The enemy wants you to think small and be filled with doubt. God wants you to think the way He does—that all things are possible to the one who has faith in His ability to work a miracle.

Read Galatians 3:5. Who gives you the Holy Spirit and works miracles? How does He work those miracles?

_____

_____

_____

_____

Does God work a miracle in your life because of what you do or what you believe? Does He do miracles because you are perfect in obeying His laws or because you believe in His ability to do the miraculous? What does that mean for you?

_____

_____

_____

Read Mark 9:39. What did Jesus say about miracles?

_____

_____

_____

Read Mark 9:23. What did Jesus say was possible, and to whom was it possible?

_____

_____

Read Mark 10:27. What is possible with God? How does that affect how you pray?

_____

_____

Read John 12:9-11. Read also page 166 in the book, the fourth paragraph. Why did the chief priests want to put Lazarus to death after Jesus worked a miracle and brought him back to life?

_____

_____

What will the enemy try to do when you pray in faith for a miracle? What will he try to do even after you receive a miracle? How should you respond to his trying to cause doubt in your heart or make you hesitant to ever pray for a miracle?

_____

_____

_____

_____

_____

Write out a prayer for some need or situation of yours or someone else's that you know would take a miracle in order for it to happen. Then leave it in God's hands to do what He wills to do.

_____

_____

_____

_____

_____

4. Resist the Enemy by Not Giving Up

Read Psalm 18:37-39. These words were spoken by David the day the Lord delivered him from his enemies. What did David do to his enemies?

_____

_____

_____

Read 2 Thessalonians 2:15. What are we to do?

_____

_____

_____

Read Colossians 4:12. What did Epaphras pray for the people?

_____

_____

_____

Write out a prayer asking God to help you stand strong against all attacks of the enemy. Ask Him to help you never give up.

_____

_____

_____

_____

Are you aware of anyone who is on the brink of giving up and needs God's help to be able to stand strong? Write out a prayer for that person.

_____

_____

_____

_____

Read Luke 18:1. Do you find yourself losing heart instead of praying when difficult things happen? Write out a prayer to God telling Him the answer to that question and asking Him to help you always turn to Him in prayer for everything.

_____

_____

_____

_____

_____

5. Resist the Enemy by Refusing to Be Discontent

Read Philippians 4:11-13. What did Paul learn how to do? Why was he able to do that?

_____

_____

_____

Read Philippians 3:8-11. What did Paul do even in the face of loss? What did he feel about what he lost? What did he believe was the most important thing?

_____

_____

_____

_____

Read Hebrews 13:5. What did Paul want the people to do and why?

_____

_____

_____

_____

_____

What does *not* being content indicate about us?

_____

_____

_____

_____

_____

Write out a prayer asking God to help you trust Him enough to know that He is always with you working in your life, and that trusting Him and being content where you are with what you have doesn't mean He is going to leave you there forever. It means you trust God in all things, and as a result, the enemy cannot lure you over to his side.

_____

_____

_____

_____

_____

6. Resist the Enemy by Remembering the Truth

Not allowing ourselves to be aligned with the enemy in any way—not taking on any of the enemy's characteristics—is part of resisting the enemy.

Read John 8:32. What is true of God's truth?

_____

_____

_____

Read John 8:44. What is true of the enemy?

_____

_____

_____

Read John 14:6. How does Jesus describe Himself?

_____

_____

_____

Read John 14:16-17. What do these verses say about the Holy Spirit?

_____

_____

_____

Read John 15:26. How is the Holy Spirit described?

_____

_____

_____

Read John 16:13. What does the Holy Spirit do?

_____

_____

_____

Write out a prayer asking God to help you remember His truth at all times. Ask Him to enable you to never speak a lie or walk according to a lie. Ask Him to help you resist the enemy by resisting all lies so that the enemy has nothing in you because you walk in the truth.

_____

_____

_____

_____

WEEK ELEVEN

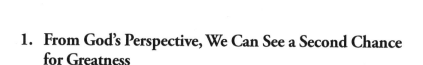

Read Chapter 11:

"See What's Happening from God's Perspective"
in *Prayer Warrior*

1. From God's Perspective, We Can See a Second Chance for Greatness

It's very important that we learn to see things from God's perspective as we prayer warriors pray because it helps us to pray more accurately. You must be able to envision how you can be a part of accomplishing great things for God through your prayers. Your life will be changed when you see that. But you don't necessarily need to have that vision *before* you start praying. In my experience, that perspective seems to grow the more you pray.

Seeing things from God's perspective happens when we read God's Word. It happens when we ask Him to show us things we need to see. It happens when we are worshipping Him.

Read page 180 in the book, the second and third paragraphs. What else does seeing things from God's perspective help us to do?

_____

_____

_____

_____

Read Romans 4:17. What is God able to do that we must always keep in mind when we pray?

_____

_____

_____

_____

Read 1 Corinthians 2:9-12. How much does God have for us? (verse 9)

_____

_____

_____

_____

If God has more for us then we can see or hear or think up on our own, then how can we ever know it? (verses 10-11)

_____

_____

_____

_____

Why have we received the Holy Spirit? (verse 12)

_____

_____

_____

_____

Read page 183 in the book, the first and second paragraphs (the first six lines). Write out these paragraphs in your own words.

_____

_____

_____

_____

_____

Read Colossians 3:1-2. What are we supposed to set our mind on?

_____

_____

_____

_____

Read page 182 in the book, the last two paragraphs. What did David do that got him into trouble?

_____

_____

_____

_____

Read Psalm 71:17-21. The psalmist, who was most likely David, asked God to do something. What was it? (verses 18)

_____

_____

_____

What did he know that God would do for him? (verses 20-21)

_____

_____

_____

_____

He knew what God could do. If God will do this for him, what will He surely do for you?

_____

_____

_____

_____

Have you ever felt as though your chance to do something great for the Lord has passed? Have you ever thought that you have been through so much, or done so many things wrong, or made such bad choices, that you cannot see how you can ever be used by God to do something great? Have you ever needed a second chance? Explain.

_____

_____

_____

_____

If God is the God of second chances, could it be that the enemy will try to stop the redemption God has for you? Write out your answer as a prayer asking God to revive you and lift you up and put His greatness in you so He can do great things through you.

_____

_____

_____

_____

_____

Write out a prayer asking God to bring you up out of the depths of whatever you have been in. (For example, despair, hopelessness, discouragement, unforgiveness, trouble, procrastination, apathy, boredom, indecision, etc.) Ask Him to help you see your future and His plans for you from His perspective.

_____

_____

_____

_____

_____

2. From God's Perspective, We See the Importance of Our Prayers

Read John 3:3. When we are born again, what begins to happen in our lives? Read also page 186 in the book, the second paragraph.

_____

_____

_____

_____

Can you think of a time when you prayed for something and your prayer wasn't answered the way you hoped it would be, but later you were able to see why it wasn't? Could you better see God's perspective in hindsight? Why was it better that God did not answer your prayer the way you prayed it?

_____

_____

_____

_____

_____

Read Galatians 6:9-10. Read also page 187 in the book, the fourth paragraph. Why should we not grow weary of praying?

_____

_____

_____

_____

Read page 188, the last paragraph. Write out a prayer asking God to help you see things from His perspective when you pray.

_____

_____

_____

_____

_____

3. From God's Perspective, We Understand the Last Days

Read 2 Timothy 3:1-7. It is important to understand the times we are in so that it is clear to us what is going on in the world. What is described in these verses that you see going on in the world today?

_____

_____

_____

_____

Read 2 Kings 6:15-17. What did Elisha say to the servant? (verse 16)

_____

_____

_____

What did the servant see? (verse 17)

_____

_____

_____

How does seeing into the invisible realm help us to believe for impossible things to happen?

_____

_____

_____

How does being able to discern spiritual things from God's perspective, and understanding God's angelic army, help you to pray?

_____

_____

_____

_____

"Overcome" is a military term that means to fight against evil forces and prevail over them. Read the following verses, and beside each one write what is promised by Jesus for those who overcome.

Revelation 2:7 _____

_____

Revelation 2:11 _____

_____

Revelation 21:7_____

_____

Read Revelation 12:11. How do we overcome? _____

_____

_____

_____

_____

The Bible will give you God's perspective on everything. The Holy Spirit will give you God's perspective on specific things He leads you to pray about, but you still need to ask Him for it. Write out a prayer asking God to reveal things to you as you pray that will help you pray in greater power.

_____

_____

_____

_____

4. From God's Perspective, We See the Right Thing to Do

In these end times we must always be able to see the truth from the lie and the right thing to do from what is wrong. If you are in the Word and walking with God in prayer, most of the time these things will be obvious, but there will be times when matters will not be so clear to you and you will need the leading of the Holy Spirit when it comes to prayer. Of course, you can always pray, "Your will be done, Lord" in every prayer. And that is a good idea. But you can also always pray, "Lead me, Holy Spirit, as I pray." And that is a good idea too.

Read Genesis 6:9–8:22. This is a long passage, but it won't take very long to read if you answer the following questions as you read it.

How full of faith was Noah? (6:9)

_____

_____

What was happening on the earth at the time of Noah? (6:11)

_____

_____

_____

What was God's perspective? (6:12-13)

_____

_____

_____

God gave specific instructions to Noah about how to build the ark, and He told him why He wanted him to build it. (6:14-17) He also told him who and what he should take with him in the boat. (6:18-21) What was the promise of God to Noah? (6:18)

_____

_____

_____

Noah was building this enormous boat nowhere near any body of water. The people around him were godless and could not see *anything* from God's perspective because they didn't know or acknowledge God. What must they have thought about what Noah was doing?

_____

_____

_____

What do you think the sinful and blinded people of Noah's generation thought about Noah when a rain of major proportions came and didn't stop? Describe what the deluge was like. (7:10-20)

_____

_____

_____

_____

_____

How old was Noah at the time? (7:11)

_____

Even for that generation, Noah was old. Do you think God can use someone in their older years—who walks closely with Him in a powerful way—to do something great for His kingdom? How does that encourage you that you can do great things as a prayer warrior for God for as long as you live? How do you think that will add to your being able to hear, "Well done, My good and faithful servant" when you see the Lord in eternity?

_____

_____

_____

_____

_____

Noah and his family and the animals were in the boat at least five months. What was the first thing Noah did when he left the ark? What did the Lord say to him? (8:20-22)

_____

_____

_____

_____

_____

Noah did the right thing because he heard from God. How important do you feel it is to hear from God in order to know how to pray as a prayer warrior? How could hearing from God as to how to pray enable you to save a life, change a life, or bring someone to life in the Lord?

_____

_____

_____

_____

Read 2 Thessalonians 2:7-12. What do these verses say about people who are blinded to the truth?

_____

_____

_____

_____

As a prayer warrior you will be praying for certain things because you are seeing them from God's perspective. Things will become so clear to you, and you will wonder why everyone doesn't see it. But other people cannot see what you see because they don't acknowledge God, Jesus, the Holy Spirit, or the Bible. Things that are happening in the world will be so obvious to you, and you will be amazed at the blindness. But only true believers who seek after God and long to see things from His perspective will see those things that are revealed to them by God in His Word and in their heart by the His Spirit in them.

Write out a prayer asking God to help you see things from His perspective as you pray so that you can do great things for Him.

_____

_____

_____

_____

_____

WEEK TWELVE

Read Chapter 12:

"Pray the Prayers Every Prayer Warrior Must Know"
in *Prayer Warrior*

Read each prayer in this chapter and the Scripture at the end of it. After each one, find the corresponding number and title here and write out a prayer for that same subject with *your own specific concerns,* either for you personally or for someone or some situation you are aware of. This will be a continuation of each prayer I have written in the book, but it will contain specific things on your heart.

1. Prayer for a Covering of Protection

Write out a prayer for you or anyone you know of who specifically needs prayer for a covering of protection over them.

_____

_____

_____

_____

_____

_____

2. Prayer for Deliverance from Evil

Write out a prayer for you or anyone you know of who specifically needs to be set free from the enemy.

_____

_____

_____

_____

_____

3. Prayer for Healing

Write out a prayer for you or anyone you know of who specifically needs prayer for healing.

_____

_____

_____

_____

_____

4. Prayer for Personal Guidance and Discernment

Write out a prayer for you or anyone you know of who specifically needs prayer to know what to do, to understand what is going on in their lives, or to have wisdom concerning something important to them.

_____

_____

_____

_____

_____

5. Prayer for Provision

Write out a prayer for you or anyone you know of who needs
God to provide for them in specific ways.

_____

_____

_____

_____

_____

6. Prayer for Victory over Enemy Attack

Write out a prayer for you or anyone you know of who needs to
be victorious in the midst of an attack of the enemy on them.

_____

_____

_____

_____

_____

7. Prayer for the Hearts of Children

Write out a prayer for your child, or anyone else's child you know of, who needs to have their heart turned toward the Lord and away from the world.

_____

_____

_____

_____

_____

8. Prayer for a Safe Place and an End to Violence

Write out a prayer for you or anyone you know of who specifically needs to find a place of safety and peace and an end to the violence around them.

_____

_____

_____

_____

_____

9. Prayer for an End to Confusion

Write out a prayer for you or anyone you know of who needs to be free of any and all confusion.

_____

_____

_____

_____

_____

10. Prayer for Freedom from Enemy Harassment

Write out a prayer for you or anyone you know of who specifically needs prayer to find freedom from enemy attack.

_____

_____

_____

_____

_____

11. Prayer for Your Leaders

Write out a prayer for any leader you know of who needs to be directed by God, or who needs to be removed from leadership because he or she is sinful and corrupt.

_____

_____

_____

_____

_____

12. Prayer for Others to Be Saved

Write out a prayer for anyone you know of who needs to have their eyes opened to the truth of Jesus and receive Him.

_____

_____

_____

_____

_____

13. Prayer for Racial Unity

Write out a prayer for anyone or any group of people you know of who need to have their eyes opened to see the need for racial unity, so that this stronghold of the enemy is broken instead of perpetuated.

_____

_____

_____

_____

_____

14. Prayer for Exaltation of God

Write out a prayer of worship, praise, and thanksgiving to God in the midst of any struggle that you or someone you know is in, because God is greater than any obstacle or enemy we face.

_____

_____

_____

_____

_____

15. Prayer for Those Who Suffer Persecution

Write out a prayer for you or anyone you know of who needs protection and freedom from persecution for their faith in Jesus.

_____

_____

_____

_____

_____

16. Prayer for a Clean Heart and Humble Spirit

Write out a prayer for you or anyone you know of who needs to have a clean heart before the Lord and to be rid of all pride.

_____

_____

_____

_____

_____

17. Prayer for Strength in the Battle

Write out a prayer for you or anyone you know of who needs to find the Lord's strength in their battle against the enemy so that they do not give up.

_____

_____

_____

_____

_____

18. Prayer for Peace in Relationships

Write out a prayer for you or anyone you know of who needs to establish strong and peaceful relationships.

_____

_____

_____

_____

_____

19. Prayer for Deliverance and Freedom

Write out a prayer for you or anyone you know of who needs to find the freedom in Christ God has for them, and deliverance from any stronghold the enemy has erected against them.

_____

_____

_____

_____

_____

20. Prayer for Serious Situations in the World

Write out a prayer about whatever serious situation you see happening in the world that needs the hand of God to intervene and turn around.

_____

_____

_____

_____

_____